Macmillan/McGraw-Hill

Online Interactive Student Book

www.macmillanmh.com

 LOG ON ▶ StudentWorks*Plus*™
Interactive Student Book

VIEW IT 👁

- Preview weekly concepts and selections

READ IT 📖

- Word-by-Word Reading

LEARN IT 🖱

- Comprehension Questions
- Research and Media Activities
- Grammar, Spelling, and Writing Activities

FIND OUT ➤

- Summaries and Glossary in other Languages

LOG ON ▶ ## Online Activities
www.macmillanmh.com

- **Interactive activities** and **animated lessons** for guided instruction and practice

 IWB Interactive White Board Ready!

D1314467

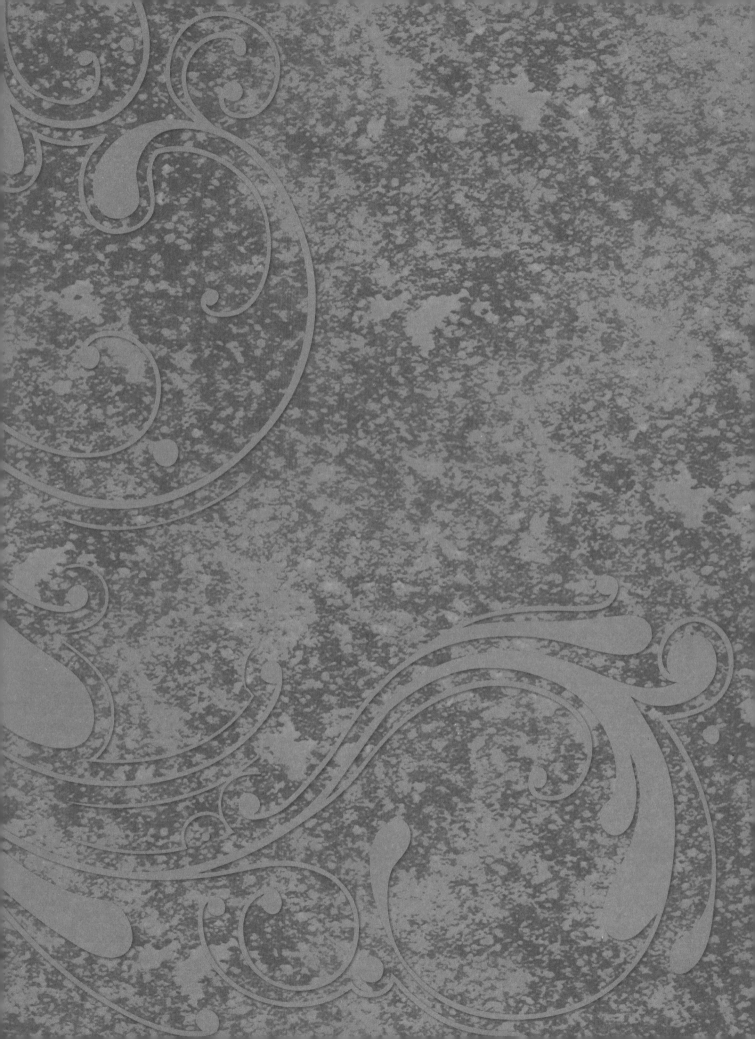

Texas Treasures

A Reading/Language Arts Program

Mc Graw Hill **Macmillan/McGraw-Hill**

Contributors

Time Magazine, Accelerated Reader

learning through listening

Students with print disabilities may be eligible to obtain an accessible, audio version of the pupil edition of this textbook. Please call Recording for the Blind & Dyslexic at 1-800-221-4792 for complete information.

B

The McGraw·Hill Companies

 Macmillan/McGraw-Hill

Published by Macmillan/McGraw-Hill, of McGraw-Hill Education, a division of The McGraw-Hill Companies, Inc., Two Penn Plaza, New York, New York 10121.

Printed in the United States of America

ISBN: 978-0-02-206155-5
MHID: 0-02-206155-X

4 5 6 7 8 9 DOW 13 12 11 10

Texas Treasures

A Reading/Language Arts Program

Program Authors

Diane August

Donald R. Bear

Janice A. Dole

Jana Echevarria

Douglas Fisher

David Francis

Vicki Gibson

Jan E. Hasbrouck

Scott G. Paris

Timothy Shanahan

Josefina V. Tinajero

Mc Graw Hill **Macmillan/McGraw-Hill**

Unit 6

Spotlight on Grade One
Adventures

The Big Question

THEME: Let's Go Out!

THEME: I Can Do It

The Big Question

What kinds of adventures can we have on any day?

LOG ON VIEW IT

Theme Video
Adventures
www.macmillanmh.com

3

What kinds of adventures can you have any day?

Have you ever had an adventure? We can have adventures every day. Sometimes adventures are fun, such as visiting a new place. Sometimes adventures can be hard, such as trying something for the first time. We can also have adventures in our imaginations. What kinds of adventures have you had?

Research Activities

Think of an adventure you have had. How was it like the adventures you are reading about? Write about how your adventure was like the one in the story.

4

Keep Track of Ideas

Use the **Layered Book Foldable** to write down your ideas about adventures. Write about the adventures you read about each week.

FOLDABLES®
Study Organizer

Adventures

Week 1

Week 2

Week 3

Week 4

Week 5

Digital Learning

LOG ON ▶ **FIND OUT** www.macmillanmh.com

StudentWorks Plus
Interactive Student Book

- **Research Roadmap**
  Follow a step-by-step guide to complete your research project.

Texas Online Resources

- Topic Finder and Other Research Tools
- Videos and Virtual Field Trips
- Photos and Drawings for Presentations
- Related Articles and Web Resources
- Texas Web Site Links

All About TEXAS

Pat Mora

Pat Mora is an author of picture books, poems, and novels. She loves to visit school children, and she founded Día, a program that promotes children's reading.

Let's Go OUT!

Talk About It

What fun places have you visited? What did you do there?

LOG ON ▶ VIEW IT

Oral Language Activities
Let's Go Out!
www.macmillanmh.com

always

mother

father

firm

supposed

love

four

***

y**ou**

t**oo**

Read to Find Out

How is Joan's bedtime like your bedtime?

Comprehension
www.macmillanmh.com

8

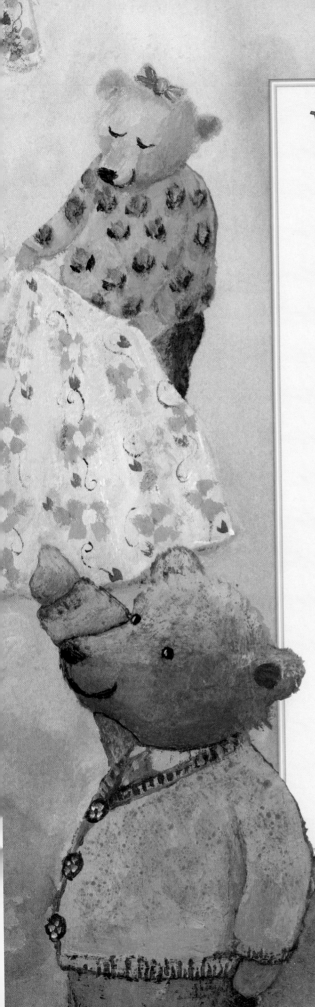

We Love Joan

Joan **always** stays up late. She likes to sing songs that she makes up. Her **mother** and **father** try to get her to sleep.

"We must be **firm** with her," her mom and dad say. "She is **supposed** to be in bed."

"Joan," says Mother, "no more songs. You must go to bed."

"We **love** you," say Mother and Father.

"I love you too," sings Joan.

She sings it **four** more times. Then she jumps into bed.

Comprehension

Genre
A Fantasy is a made-up story that could not really happen.

Visualize
Fantasy and Reality
Use your Fantasy and Reality Chart.

Reality	Fantasy
What Could Happen?	What Could Not Happen?

Read to Find Out
What kind of pig is Olivia?

OLIVIA

written and illustrated by Ian Falconer

Award Winning Author and Illustrator

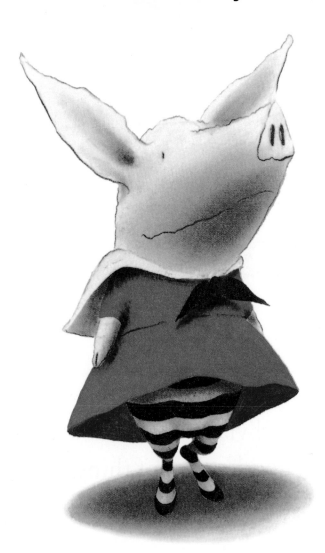

This is Olivia.
She is good at lots of things.

She is *very* good at wearing people out.

She even wears herself out.

Olivia has a little brother named Ian.
He's **always** copying.

Sometimes Ian just won't leave her alone,
so Olivia has to be **firm**.

Olivia lives with her **mother**, her **father**, her brother, her dog, Perry,

and Edwin, the cat.

In the morning, after she gets up,
and moves the cat,

and brushes her teeth,
and combs her ears,

and moves the cat,

Olivia gets dressed.

She has to try on
everything.

18

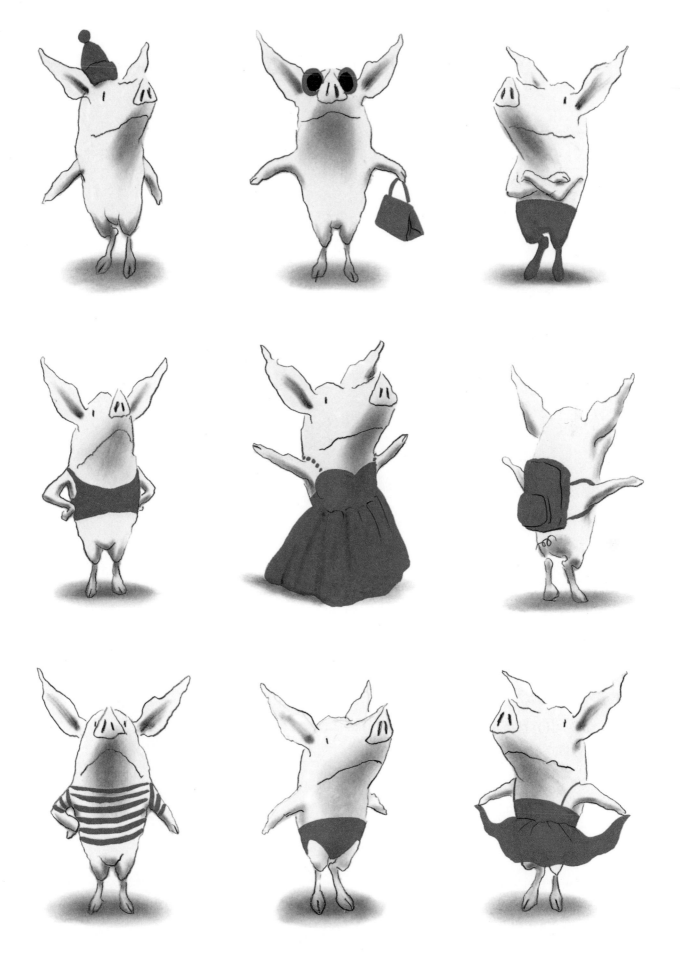

On sunny days, Olivia likes to go to the beach.

She feels it's important
to come prepared.

Last summer when Olivia was little, her
mother showed her how to make sand castles.

She got pretty good.

Sometimes Olivia
likes to bask in
the sun.

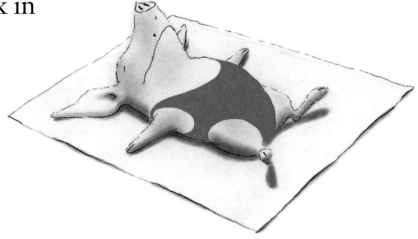

When her mother sees that she's had
enough, they go home.

Every day Olivia is **supposed** to take a nap.

"It's time for your you-know-what," her mother says.

Of course Olivia's not at all sleepy.

On rainy days, Olivia likes to go to
the museum.

She heads straight for her favorite picture.

Olivia looks at it for a long time.

What could she be thinking?

But there is one painting Olivia just
doesn't get.

"I could do that in about five minutes,"
she says to her mother.

As soon as she gets home, she gives it a try.

Time out.

After a nice bath, and a nice dinner, it's time for bed.

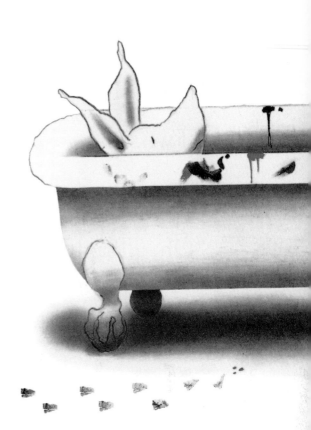

But of course Olivia's not at all sleepy.

"Only five books tonight, Mommy," she says.

"No, Olivia, just one."

"How about **four**?"

"Two."

"Three."

"Oh, all right, three.
But that's *it*!"

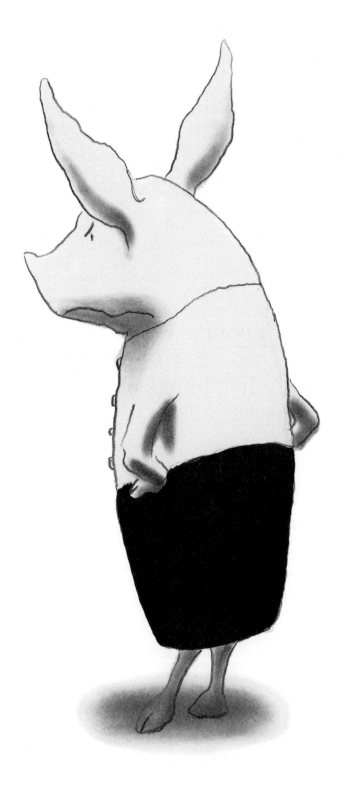

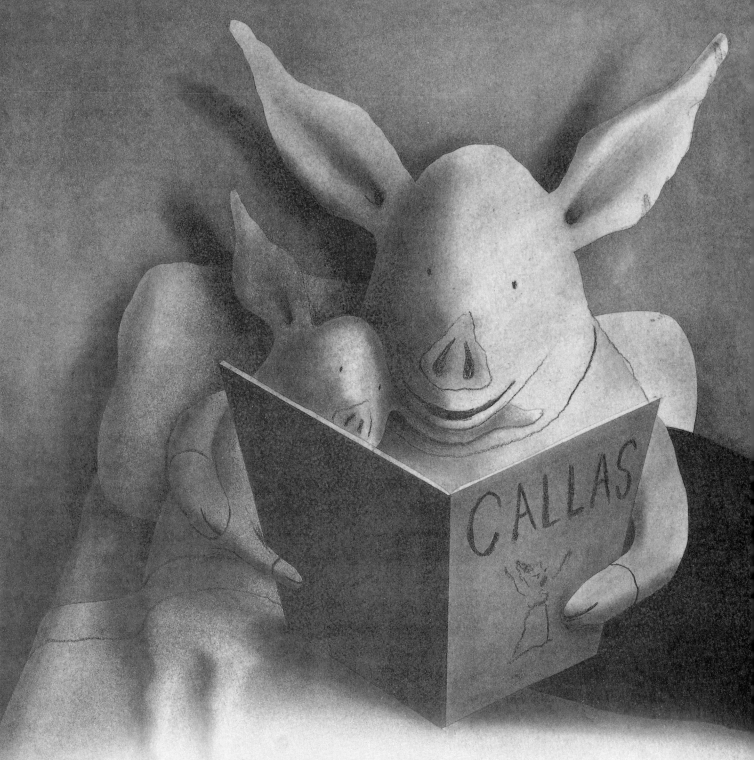

When they've finished reading, Olivia's mother gives her a kiss and says, "You know, you really wear me out. But I **love** you anyway."

And Olivia gives her a kiss back and says, "I love you anyway too."

Meet Ian Falconer

Ian Falconer says the characters in his book are based on his sister's family. His niece, Olivia, is very busy and wears out her parents, just as Olivia in the story does. He decided to make Olivia a pig because he thinks pigs are very smart animals and that they're like humans in many ways.

LOG ON ▶ FIND OUT
Author Ian Falconer
www.macmillanmh.com

Other books by Ian Falconer

OLIVIA
saves the circus

OLIVIA
...and the Missing Toy

Author's Purpose

Ian Falconer wanted to write about a smart pig. Write about another smart animal. Tell why it's smart.

TEKS Comprehension Check

Retell the Story

Use the Retelling Cards to retell the story in order.

Retelling Cards

Think and Compare

1. Who does Olivia live with?

   Details

2. Could this story happen in real life? Why or why not?

   Fantasy and Reality

3. How does Olivia's mother feel when Olivia paints on the wall? How can you tell? Character

4. How are Olivia and Joan in "We Love Joan" alike? Read Across Texts

Reality	Fantasy
What Could Happen?	What Could Not Happen?

35

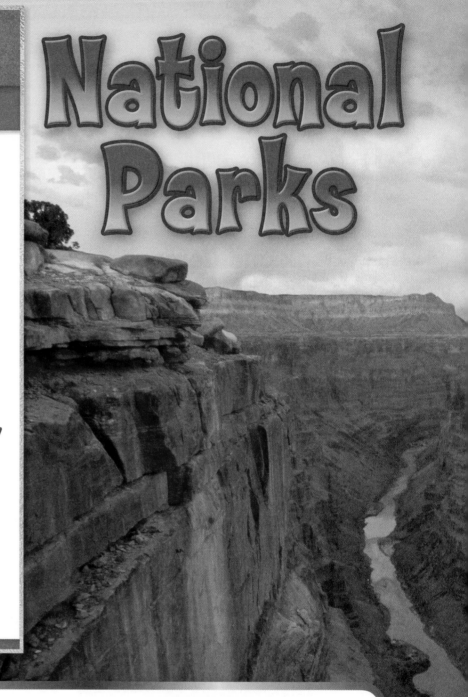

National Parks

Social Studies

Genre
Nonfiction tells about real places and things.

TEKS Text Feature
A Map is a picture that shows where places are found.

Content Vocabulary
national
border
coast

LOG ON ▶ FIND OUT

Social Studies National Parks
www.macmillanmh.com

Let's visit three of our country's **national** parks. Each is beautiful in its own way!

Grand Canyon National Park is in Arizona. Look at the layers of rock that form the Grand Canyon. The Grand Canyon is about one mile deep.

People go boating in the Rio Grande River at Big Bend. *Rio Grande* means "big river" in Spanish.

Big Bend National Park is in Texas. How did it get its name? The Rio Grande River bends, or turns, as it runs along the park's **border**.

What will you see at Big Bend? You will see the river rush between high canyon walls. You will also see deserts and mountains.

Acadia National Park is on the Atlantic Ocean.

In Maine, you can visit Acadia National Park. It's fun to walk along the rocky **coast** in summer. You can even stop and visit an old lighthouse.

Fall is a good time to visit, too. That's when the leaves change color. It is a beautiful sight!

National Parks

Use the map to find the national parks you just read about. The key tells you what the pictures or symbols mean. The scale helps you measure how far places are from one another.

TEKS Connect and Compare

- How does the key help you understand the map?
- What do the symbols on the key show?

Writing

Subjects and Predicates

The **subject** tells who or what a sentence is about. The **predicate** tells what the subject is or does.

Write a Letter

Ryan wrote to his friend about the redwood trees.

May 15

Dear Brian,
We went to see the redwood trees. The trees were as big as buildings. We drove our car through a hole in a tree! You would like it here a lot!
Yours truly,
Ryan

Your Turn

Write a letter to a classmate about a place you have been.

Tell what you saw and did.

Include a greeting, a closing, and a date.

Grammar and Writing

- Read Ryan's letter.
  Point to each **subject** and **predicate**.
  Find the date, greeting, and closing.

- Check your letter.
  Does each sentence have a **subject** and a **predicate**?
  Is there a date, a greeting, and a closing?

- Give the letter to your classmate to read.

Talk About It

What is something hard that you have learned to do? How did you learn?

Oral Language Activities
I Can Do It
www.macmillanmh.com

I Can Do It

early

instead

thought

nothing

errand

suddenly

along

saw

called

Read to Find Out

How does Cory feel at the end of the story?

LOG ON ▶ **LEARN IT**

Comprehension
www.macmillanmh.com

44

Nothing Stops Cory

Cory woke up **early**. **Instead** of going back to sleep, she got out of bed. "Today is the day I'm going to swim," she **thought**. "**Nothing** can stop me."

Mom had to do an **errand**. Then she walked Cory to the pool. **Suddenly** Cory was in the water **along** with her teacher, Shelley.

Cory held the ledge as she kicked. Then she let go and she was swimming! When she was finished, she saw her mom smile. "This is the best sport for me," Cory called.

Comprehension

Genre
Fiction is a story with made-up characters and events.

Visualize

Make Inferences
Use your Inference Chart.

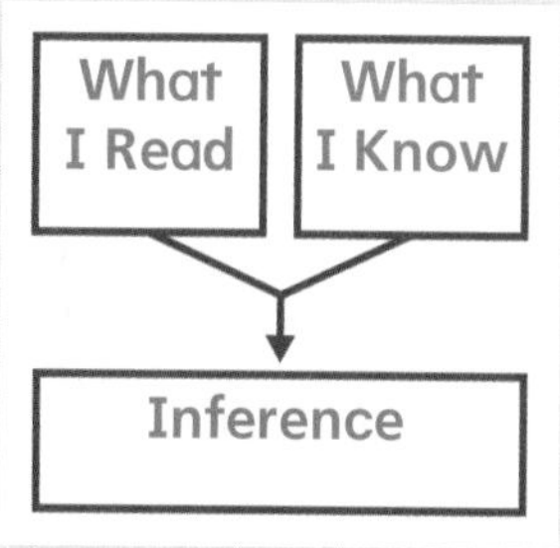

What I Read	What I Know

Inference

Read to Find Out
How does Peter feel about learning to whistle?

Whistle for Willie

by Ezra Jack Keats

Award Winning Author and Illustrator

Oh, how Peter wished he could whistle!

He saw a boy playing with his dog. Whenever the boy whistled, the dog ran straight to him.

Peter tried to whistle, but he couldn't.
So **instead** he began to turn himself around—
around and around he whirled ...
faster and faster....

When he stopped
everything turned
down …
and up …

and up …
and down …
and around
and around.

Peter saw his dog, Willie, coming.
Quick as a wink, he hid in an empty
carton lying on the sidewalk.

"Wouldn't it be funny if I whistled?" Peter **thought**.
"Willie would stop and look all around to see
who it was."

Peter tried again to whistle—but still he couldn't.
So Willie just walked on.

Peter got out of the carton
and started home.
On the way he took some
colored chalks out of his pocket
and drew a long, long line
right up to his door.

He stood there and tried to whistle again.
He blew till his cheeks were tired.
But **nothing** happened.

He went into his house and put on his father's old hat to make himself feel more grown up. He looked into the mirror to practice whistling.
Still no whistle!

When his mother saw what he was doing,
Peter pretended that he was his father.

He said, "I've come home **early** today,
dear. Is Peter here?"

His mother answered, "Why no, he's outside with Willie."

"Well, I'll go out and look for them," said Peter.

First he walked **along** a crack in the
sidewalk. Then he tried to run away
from his shadow.

He jumped off his shadow,
but when he landed they were
together again.

He came to the corner where the
carton was, and who should he
see but Willie!

Peter scrambled under the carton.
He blew and blew and blew.
Suddenly—out came a real whistle!

Willie stopped and looked around to see
who it was.

"It's me," Peter shouted, and stood up.
Willie raced straight to him.

Peter ran home to show his father and mother
what he could do. They loved Peter's whistling.
So did Willie.

Peter's mother asked him and Willie to go
on an **errand** to the grocery store.

He whistled all the way there,
and he whistled all the way home.

Getting to Know
Ezra Jack Keats

Ezra Jack Keats sold his first painting when he was eight years old! When he grew up, he created many books for children. He used cut-out paper and a special type of paste to make the bright pictures. He won many awards for his work, but he was most pleased by letters from children who had read his books.

Other books by Ezra Jack Keats

LOG ON ▶ **FIND OUT**

Author Ezra Jack Keats
www.macmillanmh.com

Author's Purpose

Ezra Jack Keats wanted to write about a boy who wished he could whistle. Write about something you wish you could do. Tell why you want to do it.

 TEKS Comprehension Check

Retell the Story

Use the Retelling Cards
to retell the story in order.

Retelling Cards

Think and Compare

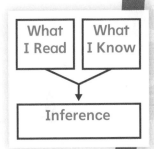

1. What does Peter wish he could do? Details

2. What happens when Peter really whistles? Sequence

3. How do you think Peter feels when he whistles? Make Inferences

4. What do Cory in "Nothing Stops Cory" and Peter both learn?

   Read Across Texts

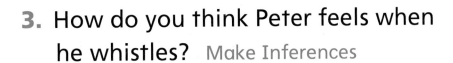

75

Social Studies

Genre
Nonfiction gives information about a topic.

 Text Feature
A List is a series of items written down in a certain order.

Content Vocabulary
guide
harness
commands

LOG ON ▶ FIND OUT

Social Studies Animals Who Help
www.macmillanmh.com

Seeing-Eye DOGS

Most dogs are pets, but some dogs have jobs. Seeing-eye dogs have a special job. They help people who can't see.

Traits of a Guide Dog

1. It is smart.
2. It likes people.
3. It is the right size.
4. It is kind.
5. It is in good shape.

Seeing-eye dogs are also called **guide** dogs. These dogs guide, or lead, blind people. The dogs can help them get anyplace they want.

How do guide dogs learn this job? Training starts when they are six weeks old. They go to live with a puppy raiser. The puppy raiser takes care of them for a year.

If a puppy shows it can learn fast, it will go to a special school. That is when the real training starts!

At school the dogs learn a lot. They get used to wearing a **harness**. They learn how to lead someone on a sidewalk. They learn how to cross a street and ride a bus. When they finish school, they can follow 20 **commands**!

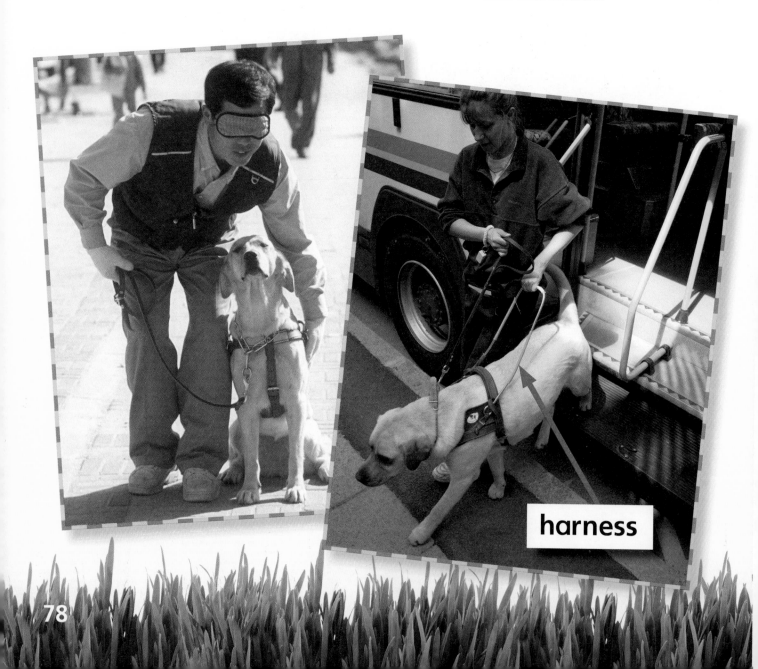

harness

Next the dog meets its new owner. They must learn how to work with each other. They train together at the school for four weeks. Then it is time to go home. They are now a team!

TEKS Connect and Compare

- What kind of guide dog do you think Willie would make?

- What did you learn from the list?

Writing

A **pronoun** is a word that replaces a noun.

Write a How-To

Ravi wrote about how to play a game.

How to Play Mix Six

1. Write a sentence. It should have six words.

2. Cut the words apart and mix them up.

3. Tell your friend to put the sentence back together.

80

Your Turn

Think of something new you have learned this year.

Think of how you learned it.

Write to explain what you learned.

Grammar and Writing

- Read Ravi's how-to.
  Explain to a partner how to play Mix Six.
  Point to each pronoun.
  Name the noun it replaces.

- Check your writing.
  Is your how-to clear and easy to use?
  What pronouns did you use?
  What nouns do they replace?

- Help a partner use your how-to.

Talk About It

What jobs do you know about? What jobs would you like to do?

Oral Language Activities
At Work
www.macmillanmh.com

At Work

interesting

only

laugh

build

goes

ordinary

<u>re</u>do

<u>un</u>happy

A Job for You

Do you ever think about what you want to be? You could find an **interesting** job. You **only** need to think about what you like!

Do you like helping people? You could be a doctor or a teacher. Do you like making people **laugh**? You could be a clown. No one would be unhappy when you are around. Do you like to make things? You could **build** new houses or redo old houses.

You could work at home. Or you could be an astronaut who **goes** to the moon. Ready, set, launch! You could want a job that seems **ordinary**, or one that does not. Think about what you like to do because then you can find your best job!

Cool Jobs

What would it be like to have these three jobs?

Zoo Dentist

If you were a zoo dentist, you could fix and clean a tiger's teeth. You could fill a hole in an alligator's tooth. You might even pull out an elephant's tusk!

Zoo dentists fix teeth just as **ordinary** dentists do. But they work on wild animals that might bite! So the dentist gives medicine to the animal. Then it **goes** to sleep. Now the dentist can get started.

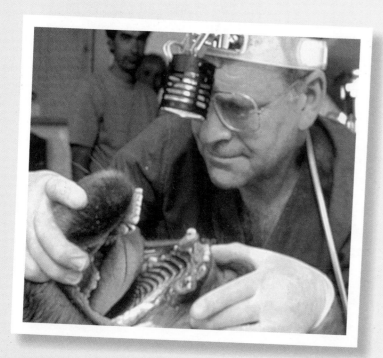

Zoo dentists use big drills to clean out holes in teeth. Big tools can help them grip a bad tooth and pull it out. If it's a lion or bear tooth, that can be a big job!

Flavor Maker

Did you ever want to change the taste of a food? If you were a flavor maker, you could! You could make medicine taste like cherry or pizza sauce. With **only** a few drops, you could cause a hot dog to taste like a peach or a pear.

Flavor makers work in a lab. They use chemicals to make flavors. Their best tools are their noses and mouths. They do a lot of tasting and smelling!

Flavor makers help make a lot of tasty food! Can you think of a new flavor for a food that you like?

Cheese-flavored crackers

Cherry-flavored medicine

Fruit-flavored cereal

89

Beekeeper

Bees make honey. A beekeeper helps the bees do their job.

If you were a beekeeper, you would **build** hives for bees to live in. These are not like the hives bees make themselves. Beekeepers make hives out of wood.

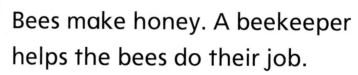

How do beekeepers remove the honey with all of those stinging bees? They have outfits to keep the bees from stinging them. There are gloves and a hood. A net protects the beekeeper's face.

Sometimes beekeepers put smoke in the hives. That makes the bees fly away. Then the beekeepers can take the honey out. It can take a lot of work to get honey. But the end is always sweet!

There are many **interesting** jobs in the world. This person's job is to dress up like a huge bird and perform at sports events. It's fun to make people **laugh**. It's hard to be unhappy when you look like a big bird!

What kinds of cool jobs can you think of? What cool job would you like?

 TEKS Comprehension Check

READ TOGETHER

Tell What You Learned

What different kinds of jobs did you learn about?

Think and Compare

1. How do zoo dentists work on wild animals without getting bitten? Details

2. What does a beekeeper do? Retell

3. Which jobs in "Cool Jobs" are about making things? Which jobs are about helping? Classify and Categorize

4. How are the jobs in "A Job for You" like the jobs in "Cool Jobs"? How are they different? Read Across Texts

Jobs at School

Would you like a job at a school? Teaching is a fun job. But there are a lot of other good jobs at school, too.

You might like to be a school nurse. A nurse takes care of sick kids. A nurse can bandage cuts and scrapes.

Do you like to fix things? You might like to be a custodian. A custodian keeps things clean. A custodian fixes things that are broken.

Do you like cooking? Then you might like a job in the lunchroom. A cook makes sure the kids have good food to eat.

There are a lot of fun jobs at school. But the best part is being with so many kids!

READ TOGETHER

DIRECTIONS
Answer the questions.

1 **This story is about jobs —**

    Ⓐ for sick kids

    Ⓑ in a lunchroom

    Ⓒ at school

2 **Who fixes your chair if it breaks?**

    Ⓐ A custodian

    Ⓑ A nurse

    Ⓒ Your teacher

3 **You can tell from this story that**

    Ⓐ many people work in schools

    Ⓑ only teachers work in schools

    Ⓒ nurses help cook good foods

READ TOGETHER

Write About an Interesting Job

Edgar wrote about a job that he thinks is interesting. He made sure his sentences were clear.

The writer told why the job is interesting.

Driving a bulldozer is a good job. Bulldozers help make roads and buildings. They are so strong. When you drive one, you get to push rocks. You can even push down buildings.

Your Writing Prompt

There are lots of different jobs.

Write a report about a job you think is interesting. Tell why it is interesting.

Writing Hints

☑ Write about what you think the job would be like. Tell why you would like it.

☑ Read your sentences over to make sure they make sense.

☑ Check your report for mistakes.

Bugs, Bugs, Bugs!

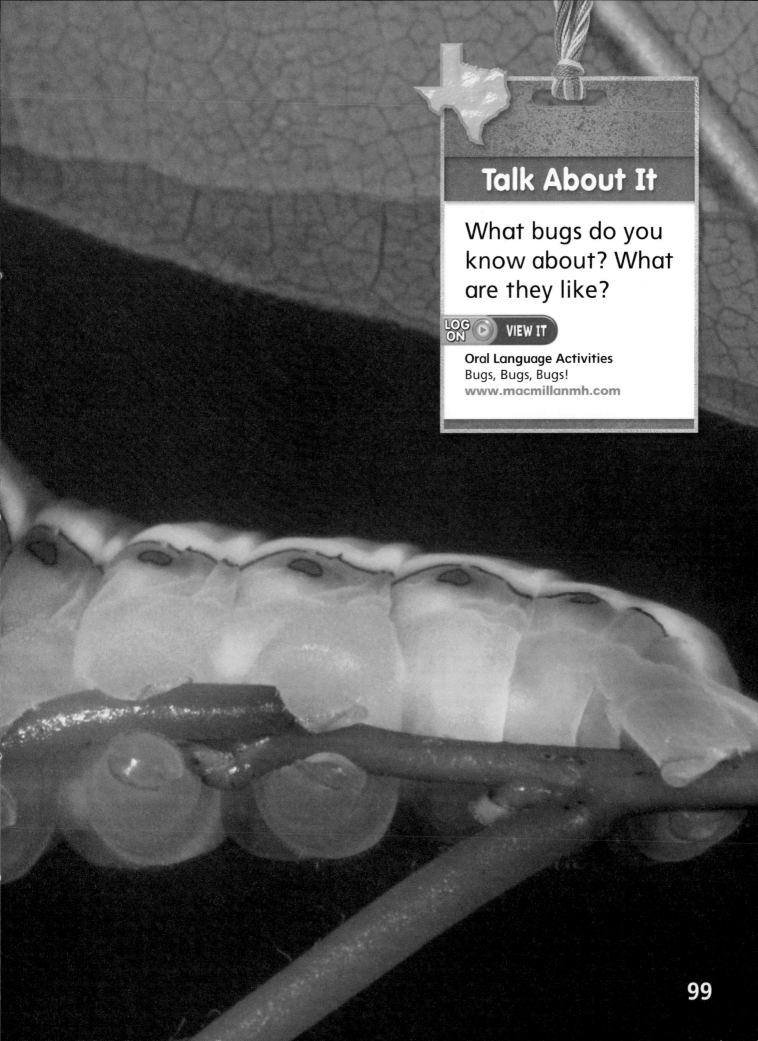

Talk About It

What bugs do you know about? What are they like?

LOG ON ▶ **VIEW IT**

Oral Language Activities
Bugs, Bugs, Bugs!
www.macmillanmh.com

gone

been

before

searching

clues

invisible

<u>sudden</u>

<u>spider</u>

Read to Find Out

How does Freddy's friend help him?

LOG ON ▶ **LEARN IT**

Comprehension
www.macmillanmh.com

Where Has Freddy Gone Now?

Fern and Freddy were best friends. So Fern was upset when she couldn't find him.

"Where has he **gone**?" she said. "He has never **been** lost **before**. I must start **searching** for him!"

Fern flew all around the pond. But she didn't find any **clues**.

"He's not **invisible**," she said.

Then there was a sudden shout. It was Freddy! He was trapped in a spider web. In a flash, Fern got him out.

"Hi," said Freddy. "Let's get out of here!" And off they went.

Comprehension

Genre

In a **Mystery**, the characters use clues to figure out something.

Reread

TEKS **Make Predictions**

Use your Predictions Chart.

What I Predict	What Happens

Read to Find Out

Where do Dot and Jabber find bugs?

Dot and Jabber
and the Big Bug Mystery

by Ellen Stoll Walsh

Award Winning
Author
and
Illustrator

Dot and Jabber, the mouse detectives, were looking for a mystery to solve. They walked through the meadow and stopped to watch some bugs.

The mice thought they heard something. They turned to see, and when they turned back, the bugs had disappeared.

"Wow," said Jabber. "The bugs vanished. Poof!"

"They must be around here someplace," said Dot. "They couldn't have **gone** away so fast."

"Then they're **invisible**," said Jabber. "I can't see them at all, and I'm looking."

"Come on, Jabber," said Dot. "This is the mystery we've **been** looking for. Let's find those bugs! We need to look for **clues**."

"Dot, listen," Jabber whispered. "I think
I hear one."

"One what?" said Dot.

"One clue. *Shhh.* Let's go check."

The mice crept over the hill.

"It's a sparrow," Jabber said. "No wonder the bugs disappeared. Sparrows eat bugs."

"Not me," the sparrow said. "I'm going to find some berries. They don't vanish when you want one."

And he hopped off.

"Now that the sparrow is gone," said Dot,
"why don't the bugs come back?"

"They're hiding from the toad," said a rabbit.
"Toads eat bugs, too."

"Where is the toad?" said Dot.

"Hiding from things that eat toads," said the rabbit.

"I don't get it," said Jabber. "Everybody's hiding, but I don't see anyplace to hide."

"Maybe we don't know how to look," said Dot. "Let's keep **searching**. The bugs can't be far away."

"They're watching us," said Jabber. "I can feel it."

"I can, too," said Dot.

"This gives me goose bumps," said Jabber. "They can see us, but we can't see them. I wonder what else is out there watching us?"

Dot caught her breath. "Jabber, quick. Something moved."

"I don't see it," said Jabber.

"Look," said Dot. "It's moving again."

Some butterflies rose from the meadow
and flew away.

"Wow, butterflies!" said Jabber. "I think the butterflies are a clue. They were hiding in plain sight, and we didn't even see them. Maybe the other bugs are hiding in plain sight, too."

"Oh!" said Dot. "Do you mean they're pretending to look like something else? Let's see if you're right."

"Dot," said Jabber. "Do rocks breathe?"

"Of course not," said Dot.

"Then I've found the toad."

"Jabber," said Dot. "I found the bugs!"

"*Shhh*," said a grasshopper.

"You're right, Dot. There are lots of bugs here!" said Jabber. "We just have to know how to look."

The grasshopper sighed. "Go ahead. Tell the toad where we are. Tell the whole world. What are a few bugs, more or less? I'm out of here."

"Wait for us!" said the other bugs.

"Well," said Dot, "the bugs have really disappeared now. But not **before** the great mouse detectives solved another mystery!" Dot looked around. "Jabber, where are you?"

"Try to find me," said Jabber. "I'm hiding in plain sight!"

Making Pictures with
Ellen Stoll Walsh

Ellen Stoll Walsh says, "We have always loved stories in my family." When she started reading stories to her son, she decided to write and make pictures for children's stories, too. She often makes the animals in her books from cut paper. She uses colored ink for her drawings.

Other books by Ellen Stoll Walsh

LOG ON ▶ FIND OUT

Author Ellen Stoll Walsh
www.macmillanmh.com

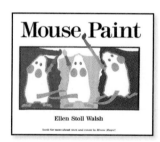

Mouse Paint

Ellen Stoll Walsh

Look for more about mice and color in *Mouse Magic!*

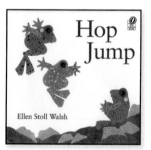

Hop Jump

Ellen Stoll Walsh

Author's Purpose

Ellen Stoll Walsh wanted to write about mice. Write about an animal you like. Tell about where it lives.

128

✓TEKS Comprehension Check

Retell the Story

Use the Retelling Cards
to retell the story in order.

Retelling Cards

Think and Compare

1. Who are Dot and Jabber?

   Details

2. What happens when Dot and
   Jabber first stop to look at the
   bugs?   Sequence

What I Predict	What Happens

3. What did you predict the bugs would
   do after Dot and Jabber found them?
   How can you tell your prediction was
   correct?   Make Predictions

4. How might Dot and Jabber look for
   Freddy in "Where Has Freddy Gone
   Now?"   Read Across Texts

Genre
Nonfiction gives information about a topic.

TEKS Text Feature
A Head tells what information is in a section.

Content Vocabulary
insects
protects
senses

The World of Insects

Insects are everywhere. There are more **insects** than any other kind of animal.

Kinds of Insects

There are all kinds of insects. The ladybug, housefly, and ant are all insects.

Some insects can fly. Many insects can not. Some live in water. But most live on the land. Some kinds of insects live and work together, such as bees or ants. But most insects do not.

The Body of an Insect

All insects have six legs. All insects have three body parts. Insect bodies have no bones. The outside of an insect's body is hard. The hard outside **protects** its insides. Many insects have antennas.

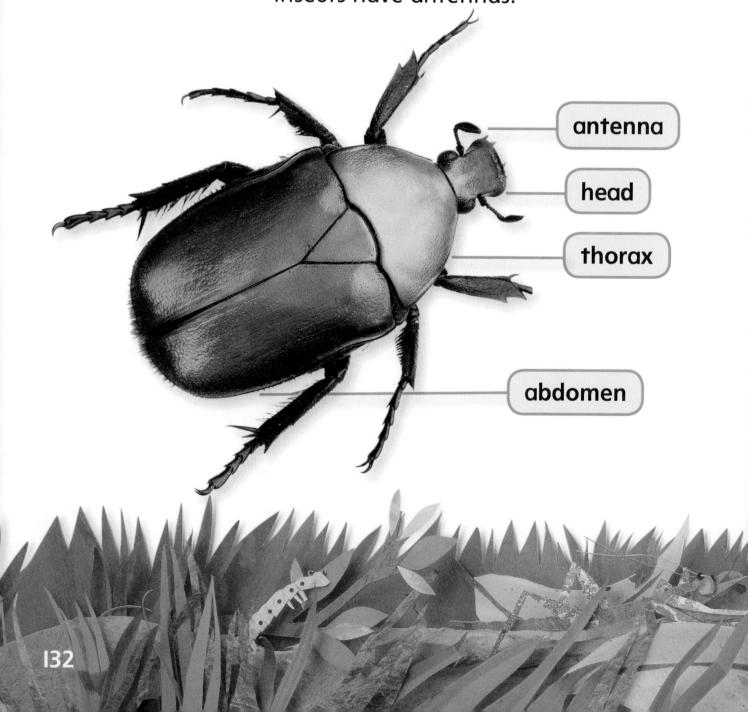

antenna

head

thorax

abdomen

Talk About It

What is a special day that you have had? What made it special?

LOG ON ▶ **VIEW IT**

Oral Language Activities
Special Days
www.macmillanmh.com

13

around

daydream

brought

straight

certain

cancel

minutes

begin

---

app<u>le</u>s

tab<u>le</u>

Read to Find Out

What will the party be like?

 **LEARN IT**

Comprehension
www.macmillanmh.com

We Like Ron!

138

The Surprise Party

Ron is my best friend. He lives **around** the corner. We play on the same team. We like to **daydream** about being baseball stars together.

Today I am having a surprise party for Ron. Ron's mom **brought** healthy snacks like apples and pears. My mom put them on the table.

We are hanging "We Like Ron!" posters. It is my job to make sure the posters are **straight**.

Phil and Shirley and Paul will be coming to the party. **Certain** grown-ups are invited too. Roy had to **cancel** because he is sick. Ron will be here in five **minutes**. Then the party will **begin**!

Comprehension

Genre
Fiction is a story with made-up characters and events.

 Reread

Character and Setting

Use your Character and Setting Chart.

Character	Setting

Read to Find Out

What happens when Oscar forgets to tell the neighbors about the picnic?

140

Super Oscar

By Oscar De La Hoya

with Mark Shulman

illustrated by Lisa Kopelke

Oscar was a daydreamer.

When Oscar rode the bus to school in the morning, he daydreamed the whole ride away. At school, Oscar would **daydream straight** through his lunchtime. And when he rode the bus home from school, he daydreamed some more.

At breakfast, Oscar daydreamed as his
pancakes got cold and his orange juice
got warm.

His father said, "Oscar, it's good to dream.
But sometimes you need to take your head
out of the clouds to get things done."

"Right," Oscar said.

On Saturdays in Oscar's neighborhood, everyone got together for a picnic in the park. People **brought** all sorts of food and there were games to play.

Oscar's mother was in charge of making the lists so that everyone knew what to bring. Oscar would run **around** his neighborhood to give out the lists. One week a **certain** daydreamer forgot to give them out.

That Saturday, Oscar was lying on the grass, looking at the shapes in the clouds.

His mother called, "OSCAR! You never gave out the lists! We'll have to **cancel** the picnic. There won't be anything to eat!"

"Don't worry, Mami!" Oscar said as he jumped up. "There's still time!"

149

And in a flash, Oscar zipped away. He rushed
to the grocery store. He bought everything
he needed and raced to the park.

Twenty minutes until the picnic....

Oscar quickly unpacked the groceries and set the picnic tables.

Fifteen minutes until the picnic....

Next, Oscar made up a humongous batch
of guacamole following Tía Raquel's
recipe ... for the most part.

Ten minutes until the picnic....

Then Oscar began whipping up the cream
for the strawberry shortcake dessert.

Five minutes until the picnic....

The clock struck noon. It was time for the picnic to **begin**. All of Oscar's friends and neighbors came into the park. Oscar was excited—until he realized there was no music!

154

Oscar taught a few friends a tune. They performed it beautifully as everyone was arriving at the picnic site.

This picnic started with Oscar's favorite event—the empanada-eating contest.

It was the best picnic ever.

By the time the strawberry shortcake was served that afternoon, Oscar was nowhere to be found.

Sweet dreams, Oscar.

Meet the Real Super Oscar

The real Oscar De La Hoya is a super athlete. He is famous all over the world for his skill in boxing. As a child Oscar went to school in East Los Angeles. His real dream is to make good schools for kids from that neighborhood. Like Oscar in the story, he has a lot of energy and likes to help out!

LOG ON ▶ FIND OUT

Author Oscar De La Hoya
www.macmillanmh.com

Author's Purpose

The real Super Oscar likes to take on big challenges. Write about another challenge little Super Oscar could take on.

TEKS Comprehension Check

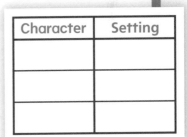

Retell the Story

Use the Retelling Cards to retell the story in order.

Retelling Cards

Think and Compare

Character	Setting

1. What word does the author use to describe Oscar? Character

2. Why does Oscar get the picnic ready by himself? How does he do it? What places does he go? Character and Setting

3. Could this story happen in real life? Why or why not? Fantasy and Reality

4. How is Oscar's day like the children's day in "The Surprise Party"? Read Across Texts

LOG ON ▶ FIND OUT

Poetry

Genre
Poetry uses rhythm and rhyme to make words fun to say.

TEKS **Literary Element**
Many poems have a **Rhyming Pattern**. In some poems, the second line in a verse rhymes with the fourth line.

Poetry Rhyming Patterns
www.macmillanmh.com

DANCING PAPER

by Pat Mora

Let's fill the room with laughing
before our friends arrive.
We'll bring the colored paper.
The room will come alive.

Let's start with the *piñata*.
The air will sway and swing.
We'll string *papel picado*
to start its fluttering.

164

I'll fling the *serpentinas*,
toss coils in the air.
We'll add *marimba* music,
start dancing everywhere.

Remember *cascarones*,
to hide will be in vain.
Egg-bursts of bright confetti
will shower us like rain.

TEKS Connect and Compare

- How is the special day in *Super Oscar* like the day described in "Dancing Paper"?

- What lines in this poem rhyme?

Writing

Adverbs

Adverbs tell more about a verb. Some adverbs end in *-ly*.

Write a Letter

Isabel wrote a letter about a special day.

June 16

Dear Devi,

Today my brother came home. We had a party. I helped cook and hang up decorations. Then he came in. "Welcome Home!" we shouted loudly. He was so surprised!

Your friend,

Isabel

Welcome Home!

166

Your Turn

Think about a special day you have had.

Write a letter to a friend. Write what you did on that special day.

Include the date, a greeting, and a closing.

Grammar and Writing

- Read Isabel's letter.
  Point to the **adverb** that ends in *-ly.*
  What verb does it tell about?

- Check your letter.
  Is there a date, a greeting, and a closing?
  Will it make sense to your reader?
  Do you use **adverbs** correctly?

- Read your letter to a partner.

Review

Character and Setting
Make Predictions
Context Clues
Captions
Chart

THE Picnic Tent

Jen and James packed a picnic for the park. They put peanut butter and jelly sandwiches and drinks in a basket. Jen put their lunch and a plastic tablecloth on her bike. James put their kites, a ball, and two books of mazes in his backpack.

At the park, Jen and James flew their kites. They played catch. But then it began to rain.

"It's too soon to go home," said James.

Jen knew what to do. She removed the plastic cloth from the table. She put it under the table. Then she and James ate lunch and did mazes until it stopped raining.

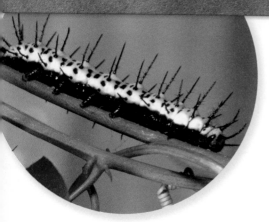

Life of a Butterfly

Where do butterflies come from? A butterfly begins life as an egg. When the egg hatches, a caterpillar crawls out. It crawls on leaves and it uses them for food. As it eats, it grows. As it gets bigger, it changes in other ways.

The caterpillar hangs upside down from a leaf or a stalk. Next, it makes a hard shell around itself. Inside, the caterpillar changes more. Now it is called a pupa.

In about ten days, the pupa's shell cracks. A butterfly comes out. At first its wings are wet. When its wings dry, the butterfly flies away. It begins a new life.

Most butterflies live from one to two weeks. Some may live for a year.

A Butterfly's Life

1 Egg	
2 Caterpillar	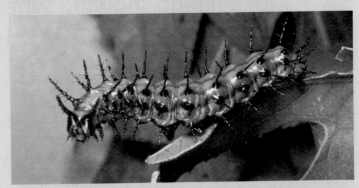
3 Pupa	
4 Butterfly	

 Comprehension

Treasure Hunt

- Make a treasure map.

  First draw something special. Hide it in your classroom.

- Make a map showing where to find your treasure. Mark the spot with an "x."

- Use signs and symbols for doors, desks, cubbies, and other classroom features.

- Create a key that tells what your signs and symbols mean. Exchange maps with a classmate. Look for treasure.

 Word Study

Find the Words

- Read the sentence.

  The red hen ate quickly.

- Find the adjective and the adverb.

- Write a sentence. Have a partner find the adjectives and adverbs.

Writing

Write a Letter

- Write a letter to a friend. Tell about an adventure you had in first grade.

- Make sure your letter will make sense to your reader. Tell what happened in order.

- Begin your letter with a greeting and end it with a closing. Include a date.

Write a Sound Poem

- Write a classroom sound poem.

- Close your eyes. Listen carefully. What do you hear in your classroom? What do you hear outside? What do you think is making those sounds?

- Write a poem describing the sounds. You may want to use sound words.

Glossary

What Is a Glossary?

A glossary can help you find the meanings of words. The words are listed in alphabetical order. You can look up a word and read it in a sentence. Sometimes there is a picture.

insects

coast

Sample Entry

Letter

S s

Main Entry

straight

Sentence

The ruler is a helpful tool for drawing a **straight** line.

around

Aa

along

The boys hiked **along** a river.

always

Paul **always** arrives late.

around

We like to ride **around** and around.

Bb

been

The boys were dirty because they had **been** playing in the mud.

before

Before he throws the ball, the player jumps as high as he can.

begin

When fall starts, leaves **begin** to pile up in the yard.

border

Mexico is on the southern **border** of the United States. Canada is on the northern **border.**

brought

Kit **brought** her little brother with her.

build

Beavers **build** dams in ponds and rivers.

Cc

cancel

If it rains, we'll **cancel** the picnic.

certain

Certain cats come when you call them.

clues

The **clues** helped Jim solve the mystery.

coast

We walked along the rocky **coast** and looked at the ocean.

commands

Trained dogs learn to follow **commands**.

Dd

daydream

Try not to **daydream** in class.

Ee

early

Pete wakes us **early** in the morning.

errand

Tom ran an **errand** for his mom.

Ff

father

Jack and his **father** are cooking dinner.

firm

The teacher is **firm** about the rules.

four

There are **four** slices of bread left.

Gg

goes

A train **goes** fast.

gone

The pickles are all **gone**.

guide

The **guide** took our class through the museum.

Hh

harness

That **harness** is for the brown horse.

Ii

insects
All **insects** have six legs and three body parts.

instead
I chose the red shirt **instead** of the blue one.

interesting
I read an **interesting** book.

invisible
The brown lizard is almost **invisible** on the sand.

Ll

laugh
We **laugh** a lot when we are together.

love

I **love** my pet.

Mm

minutes

There are 60 **minutes** in an hour.

mother

My **mother** always braids my hair.

Nn

national

There is a **national** election for president every four years.

nothing

I bought **nothing** at the store.

Oo

only

There was **only** one pencil left.

ordinary

On an **ordinary** day, Maya plays outside after school.

Pp

protects

An umbrella **protects** me from the rain.

Ss

searching

I spent a long time **searching** for my sock.

senses

You use your five **senses** to taste, smell, see, hear, and touch.

straight

The ruler is a helpful tool for drawing a **straight** line.

suddenly

Suddenly the room got dark.

supposed

I am **supposed** to go to bed early.

Tt

thought

He **thought** hard when he took the test.

Acknowledgments

The publisher gratefully acknowledges permission to reprint the following copyrighted material:

"Dancing Paper" from *Confetti: Poems for Children* by Pat Mora. Text copyright © 1996 by Pat Mora. Reprinted with permission of Lee & Low Books, Inc.

Dot & Jabber and the Big Bug Mystery by Ellen Stoll Walsh. Text and illustrations copyright © 2003 by Ellen Stoll Walsh. Reprinted by permission of Harcourt, Inc.

Olivia by Ian Falconer. Copyright © 2000 by Ian Falconer. Reprinted by permission of Atheneum Books for Young Readers, an imprint of Simon & Schuster Children's Publishing Division.

Super Oscar by Oscar De La Hoya, illustrated by Lisa Kopelke. Text copyright © 2006 by Oscar De La Hoya. Illustrations copyright © 2006 by Lisa Kopelke. Used with permission of Simon & Schuster Books for Young Readers, an imprint of Simon & Schuster Children's Publishing Division.

Whistle for Willie by Ezra Jack Keats. Text and illustrations copyright © 1964 by Ezra Jack Keats. Reprinted by permission of the Penguin Group, a division of Penguin Putnam Books for Young Readers.

Book Cover, HOP JUMP by Ellen Stoll Walsh. Copyright © 1993 by Ellen Stoll Walsh. Reprinted by permission of Harcourt Brace & Company.

Book Cover, GOGGLES! by Ezra Jack Keats. Copyright © 1969 by Ezra Jack Keats. Reprinted by permission of Viking, an imprint of Penguin Putnam Books for Young Readers.

Book Cover, MOUSE PAINT by Ellen Stoll Walsh. Copyright © 1989 by Ellen Stoll Walsh. Reprinted by permission of Harcourt Brace & Company.

Book Cover, OLIVIA AND THE MISSING TOY by Ian Falconer. Copyright © 2003 by Ian Falconer. Reprinted by permission of Atheneum Books for Young Readers, an imprint of Simon & Schuster Children's Publishing Division.

Book Cover, OLIVIA SAVES THE CIRCUS by Ian Falconer. Copyright © 2001 by Ian Falconer. Reprinted by permission of Atheneum Books for Young Readers, an imprint of Simon & Schuster Children's Publishing Division.

ILLUSTRATIONS
Cover Illustration: Pablo Bernasconi

8–9: Tiphanie Beeke. 10–35: Ian Falconer. 40: Ken Bowser. 44–45: Michael-Che Swisher. 46–75: Ezra Jack Keats. 100–101: Will Terry. 102–129: Ellen Stoll Walsh. 130–133: Susan Swan. 134: Rachel Geswaldo. 138–139: Holli Conger. 140–163: Lisa Kopelke. 164–165: Susan Swan. 166: Jenny Vainisi. 168–169: Janee Trasler.

PHOTOGRAPHY
All photographs are by Ken Cavanagh or Ken Karp for Macmillan/McGraw Hill (MMH) except as noted below.

iv: Jason Lindsey/Alamy. v: Photodisc/PunchStock. 2–3: Jason Lindsey/Alamy. 4: Comstock Images. 4–5: Royalty-Free/Corbis. 5: Cheron Bayna. 6–7: Jiang Jin/SuperStock. 25: (c) Réunion des Musées Nationaux/Art Resource, NY. 27: © The Metropolitan Museum of Art/Art Resource, NY & © 2010 The Pollock-Krasner Foundation/Artists Rights Society (ARS), New York. 34: Courtesy of Roddy McDowell. 36–37: Momatiuk-Eastcott/Corbis. 37: Michael Melford/Getty Images. 38: (cr) Karl Kinne/PhotoLibrary; (t) James Randklev/Corbis. 40: George Shelley/Corbis. 41: Johner/Getty Images. 42–43: Jeff Cadge/Getty Images. 74: Courtesy of Ezra Jack Keats. 76: Digital Vision/Getty Images. 76–77: (b) Westend61/Alamy. 77: Paul Doyle/Alamy. 78: (l) Richard Sobol/Animals Animals; (r) Phanie/Photo Researchers. 78–79: (b) Westend61/Alamy. 79: tbkmedia.de/Alamy. 80: Stephen Simpson/Getty Images. 81: S.Meltzer/PhotoLink/Getty Images. 82–83: Photodisc/PunchStock. 84–85: Zephyr Picture/Index Stock. 85: Jose Luis Pelaez, Inc./Corbis. 86: Tim Wimbourne/Reuters/NewsCom. 87: (tr) Steve Hart. 88: (all) Janet Worne/Lexington Herald-Leader/KRT/NewsCom. 89: (tr) JupiterImages/AbleStock/Alamy; (cr,tl) Burke Triolo Productions/Getty Images; (b) Richard Smith/Masterfile; (cl) Royalty-Free/Corbis. 90: (tc) Stefan Sollfors/Alamy; (tr) Burke/Triolo Productions/Brand X Pictures/Getty Images; (cr) G.K. & Vikki Hart/Getty Images; (tl) Independence Examiner, Margaret Clarkin/AP Images; (tcr) JupiterImages/Creatas/Alamy; (b) JupiterImages/Photos.com/Alamy; (bl) Stefan Sollfors/Alamy. 91: (tr) Rich Pedroncelli/AP Images; (c) Stefan Sollfors/Alamy; (bcl) Julie Toy/Getty Images; (bc) Maximilian Stock-StockFood Munich/Stockfood America; (br) G.K. & Vikki Hart/Getty Images; (bl) Burke/Triolo Productions/Brand X Pictures/Getty Images. 92: Creatas/Jupiter Images. 92–93: Steve Craft/Masterfile. 93: (bl) Photolink/Getty Images; (br) William Fritsch/Brand X Pictures/JupiterImages. 94: Richard Lord/The Image Works. 96: Digital Vision. 97: (bc) Bet Noire/Shutterstock; (c, br) C Squared Studios/Getty Images. 98–99: Patti Murray/Animals Animals. 128: Courtesy of Ellen Stoll Walsh. 130: (c) Burke/Triolo Productions/Brand X Pictures/Getty Images; (br) Photodisc/Getty Images. (cr) Ingram Publishing/Alamy. 131: (t) Charles Krebs/Getty Images; (tr) Ron Wu/Index Stock Imagery; (cl) Burke/Triolo Productions/Brand X Pictures/Getty Images; (cr) Dynamic Graphics Group/Creatas/Alamy; (bl) Brian Hagiwara/Jupiter Images; (br) Bob London/Corbis. 132: (tl) Werner H. Müller/Corbis; (c) Brian Hagiwara/Brand X/Corbis. 133: (tr) Anthony Bannister/Gallo Images/Corbis; (c) IT Stock Free/AGE Fotostock. 134: BananaStock/PunchStock. 135: Digital Archive Japan/PunchStock. 136–137: Masterfile Royalty-Free. 162: J.P. Yim/Zuma/Corbis. 166: Image Source/PunchStock. 167: Creatas/PunchStock. 170: (tl) E. R. Degginger/Photo Researchers; (br) Gail Shumway/Getty Images. 171: (t to b) David M. Dennis/Animals Animals; David Liebman/Pink Guppy; David M. Dennis/Animals Animals; Margarette Mead/Getty Images. 172: (bc) Stephen Ogilvy/Macmillan McGraw-Hill; (br) Royalty Free/Corbis. 173: Nic Hamilton/Alamy. 174: (cr) Burke/Triolo Productions/Brand X Pictures/Getty Images; (l) Dave Reede/Getty Images. 175: (t) Corbis/Superstock; (b) Rommel/Masterfile. 176: Rommel/Masterfile. 177: Photolink/Getty Images. 178: Dave Reede/Getty Images. 179: Ariel Skelley/Corbis. 180: Photographer's Choice/Getty Images. 181: (b) Peter Hince/Getty Images; (b) Burke/Triolo Productions/Brand X Pictures/Getty Images. 182: Royalty-Free/CORBIS. 183: Jim Cummins/Getty Images. 184: Corbis/Superstock.